MW00936067

A Kids Guide to Mission San Juan Capistrano:

ekids Press

www.eKidsPress.com

An Imprint of Minute Help, Inc.

© 2012. All Rights Reserved.

Table of Contents

ABOUT EKIDS 3

INTRODUCTION 5

CHAPTER 1: THE PURPOSE OF THE MISSION 8

CHAPTER 2: HISTORY OF THE MISSION PERIOD ...10
   REBUILDING SAN JUAN CAPISTRANO 11
   PROSPEROUS, YET DIFFICULT TIMES 14

CHAPTER 3: HISTORY OF THE RANCHO PERIOD ...17
   DISBANDING THE MISSION 18
   A SECULAR TOWN 20

CHAPTER 4: HISTORY OF THE CALIFORNIA
STATEHOOD 23

CHAPTER 5: WHAT WAS LIFE ON THE MISSION LIKE
DURING THE MISSION PERIOD?....................................28
   IMPORTS..30
   DAILY WORK...31
   IMPORTANT INDUSTRIES FOR TRADE 36
   HOW DID THEY GET WATER? 38
   LIVING ARRANGEMENTS 39
   RELIGION AND LEARNING...40
   MARRIAGES AND OTHER CEREMONIES......................43
   WHAT KINDS OF FOOD DID THEY EAT? 45
   GAMES AND FUN..48
   MEDICINE AND HEALING 50
   THE MISSION BELLS 52

CHAPTER 6: MODERN DAY 57

CONCLUSION...61

ADDITIONAL RESOURCES 62

About eKids

Adults! Turn away! This book is not for you!

eKids Books is proud to present a new series of books for all the readers who matter the most: Kids, of course!

Introduction

Have you ever heard about the Mission San Juan Capistrano? If you haven't, or even if you have, you may not know much about it. America has a lot of history and many of its stories are probably new to you. The story of this mission is filled with twists and turns, so get ready for an exciting tale that starts way back in the late 1700s and is still unfolding today!

First of all, this Catholic mission was actually founded twice, which means that is was settled once and started up, only to fall victim to fears of a massive attack. The original settlement of San Juan Capistrano was on October 30, 1775 by Father Fermín Lasuén. This was the brainchild of Father Junipero Serra, who believed that the mission should be founded in order to break up the long journey between San Diego and San Gabriel. He named it after a very famous 15th century theologian and "warrior priest" from Italy named San Juan Capistrano.

The mission was only running for a mere eight days when they heard word that a neighboring mission had been attacked by the Native Americans. Everyone on the mission was very fearful that this could happen again and they were not sure exactly what they should do. They decided that in order to avoid serious unrest among the indigenous population in the area and a possible dangerous attack on the people of the mission, all of the padres (Fathers) and the soldiers in the mission should flee to San Diego and bury the mission bells. When Father Serra made his way to Alta one year later, he uncovered the bells and once again rang them for the Mission San Juan Capistrano.

The Mission San Juan Capistrano was founded for a second time on November 1, 1776 by Father Serra. November 1st is an important day because it is a holiday in the Catholic faith known as "All Saints Day." This day is to recognize the Saints of the Catholic faith, which is why Father Serra felt that the re-founding of the Mission San Juan Capistrano would be blessed if it was done on this day. Father Serra's Mission was the 7th mission in a long line of 21 missions in the Alta region of California.

The Mission San Juan Capistrano joined the ranks of other missions that were founded during the late 1700s. These missions all had the same goal (you'll find out more about that in the next section) and were a large part of the history and culture of California. Many of these missions left a lasting legacy on the area, including San Juan Capistrano, and the structures that they built still stand today. You will be surprised at what life was like on the mission, and the story that is about to unfold about the Mission San Juan Capistrano will hopefully give you a clearer picture of how California was settled and about one of the many missions that thrived for a number of years in the area.

Chapter 1: The Purpose of the Mission

Why were missions being started all over California at this time? These missions were an integral part of the founding and settling of California. The purpose was simple: to spread the word of Christianity to the natives in California and neighboring Mexico. Father Serra and the other leaders of the mission sought to build a safe refuge for all those who lived in the area and wanted to bring their beliefs to people who might never have heard of them before. They believed that forming a peaceful settlement that was centered around the church would bring the natives and the new settlers together as a strong and lasting community.

Their goal was to establish a place to live where the beliefs of the church would be the integral part of the area. The natives, as well as the Fathers who were running the church, would spend much of their days learning, studying and discussing the Bible. They would also farm the land and provide for themselves in terms of food and shelter. They would build a massive church, where everyone in the area would gather and share a sense of faith and community. They would also raise families and spread their Christian legacy for many generations to come.

Chapter 2: History of the Mission Period

The Mission Period at San Juan Capistrano lasted from 1769-1833. It was during this time that the mission was established and built up to become a thriving and fully sufficient settlement. Many of the early years were spent struggling to find a balance and getting everything settled and the important buildings erected.

Once the mission site had been chosen and re-founded by Father Serra in 1776, it was time to begin construction. When the first mission was settled in 1775, an arbor was constructed, two bronze bells were hung from the branch of a tree that was nearby, and a wooden cross was planted. When the first settlement fled among fears of a serious attack on the mission, they buried the bells and took their remaining possessions. The priests and the Spanish soldiers left the area in a hurry, only to hear of even more disasters in surrounding missions when they were safe at the Presido.

Rebuilding San Juan Capistrano

The next year, Father Serra and two other Fathers returned to the Mission San Juan Capistrano. They had eleven Spanish soldiers with them and they set about getting the mission back up and running. They dug up the bells and hung them from a new arbor that they constructed. The original wooden cross was still there, standing proud and tall, which they saw as a positive sign for their new mission. Father Serra conducted a High Mass ceremony on November 1, 1776, which was considered the founding day of the Mission San Juan Capistrano.

Unfortunately, it was found very soon that there was not enough water in the area for the mission to be successful. You know how important water is to your life, and the founders of the Mission San Juan Capistrano knew this as well. They moved the mission three short miles away, where they had better access to the fresh water that they needed. They were now very close to an Indiana village that was inhabited by the Acágcheme tribe.

The new site of the mission was now equipped with the water that they needed from two streams that were very close by, which were called the San Juan and the Trabuco. The mission at San Gabriel offered cattle to the new mission, as well as Native American labor to help with getting the mission up and running.

The very first baptism on the mission was performed on that first year of settlement on December 19. In fact, during the years 1776 and 1847 nearly 5,000 people were baptized at the Mission San Juan Capistrano. The very first chapel, which was called an adobe capilla, was blessed in 1778. This building was replaced by a much larger house of worship in 1782 and is the oldest building in California today. It is called the Serra Chapel. By the time of the completion of the large chapel in 1782, many other buildings on the mission grounds had been completed. There were now storerooms, workshops, soldiers' barracks, kitchens, and living quarters that made up what was known as the main quadrangle of the mission.

The very first Vineyard in all of California was also planted during the early days of the mission. The "Mission" grape was planted in 1779 and these continued to be grown throughout Spanish America. The first official winery in Alta California was also built at San Juan Capistrano in 1783.

In 1791, the original bells of the mission were removed from where they had been hanging and were mounted, further solidifying the establishment of the mission as an important place in California.

Prosperous, Yet Difficult Times

Are you amazed at the amount of work that was put into the mission just to get it going? All of the hard work paid off for the Fathers and the native people in the area, as by 1794 more than seventy permanent housing structures were built for the mission Indians. These were made of adobe. As you can see, the population of the mission was growing rapidly and the previous church was just not large enough to accommodate everyone in the mission. Because of this, the "Great Stone Church" was constructed. The church was made with a domed roof made of stone and was made to look like a classic Greco-Roman church with elaborate decorations and columns. It was actually laid out in the shape of a cross and was the only chapel building in Alta California that was not made out of adobe. Construction was a long, hard process, as you can surely imagine. Work began on February 2, 1797, but was not completed until 1806. There were many setbacks during construction, including an earthquake in 1800 that cracked the walls, leading to many extra repairs.

Earthquakes would continue to pose a problem throughout the rest of the Mission period. California is rife with earthquakes and on December 8, 1812, the well-established mission settlement was shook to their core when the huge Wrightwood Earthquake struck the area. This was a 7.0 magnitude quake, which is enough to completely topple an entire town. Much of the great church was damaged, as well as many of the settlement homes. The farmlands flooded as well, as more buildings were damaged and more than 40 people lost their lives. The Great Stone Church was never fully rebuilt after the quake.

Throughout the next 10 years or so, the mission was plagued by disease, problems with crops and Spanish settlers that sought to take over the fertile land of San Juan Capistrano. A large majority of the Indian population left and this lead to a massive deterioration of the land. Mexico gained independence from Spain in 1821, leading even more of the Native Americans to leave the area. The Mexicans did not want their native people being forced to work on the missions, which led them to do everything in their political power to free their people from the land of Southern California. In 1826, all Native Americans within most of Southern California were made free Mexican citizens, further influencing them to leave the missions. Eventually on August 17, 1833, the Mexican Congress passed <u>An Act for the Secularization of the Missions of California</u>, which essentially shut down the Mission San Juan Capistrano. The Act provided for Alta and Baja California to be colonized and the mission land to be sold.

Chapter 3: History of the Rancho Period

The Rancho Period is the period of time after Mexico had won independence from Spain and had ended the missions in Southern California. The Rancho Period was from 1834-1849, which many people call the secularization period. During this time, all of the missions in Southern California were completely taken apart and the majority of the people that had lived there and worked there left. Most of these people were now freed Mexicans who had resided there (some against their will), so they were happy to be freed. The others that departed were the Franciscan Catholics, many of who went back to Spain or to other parts of America after they lost their Mission land.

Disbanding the Mission

On November 22, 1834, Commissioner Juan Jose Rocha acknowledged the receipt of the Decree of Confiscation and then the inventory of the Mission San Juan Capistrano was compiled so that it could all be sold. The Mexican government had won the war with Spain and had therefore become the owners of the land that the Mission San Juan Capistrano was on. It was a sad time for the leading Fathers who had truly believed in the mission. The inventory consisted of all of the items that could be sold off from the mission for monetary gain. There were many buildings, the chapel, furnishings, tools, ranch lands, library holdings, and large amounts of agricultural holdings. The agriculture that was to be sold off included 8,000 cattle, 4,000 sheep, 50 horses, 80 pigs, 9 mules, maize, beans, and large amounts of wine and brandy.

After the inventory was taken, nearly all of the Franciscan priests abandoned the mission. Many of the locals came to the mission and stole construction materials from the buildings that were left, leaving very little of the mission settlement intact. The area became all but a ghost town. The population at San Juan Capistrano in 1834 had dropped to only 861 people, and in 1840 this was reduced to less than 500. The crops had nearly completely deteriorated and little was left of the once thriving Mission San Juan Capistrano except for the memories in the hearts of those who had lived there.

While this was a difficult time for the Fathers and the many people who believed in the mission, it was a happy time for the Native Americans who were no longer forced to work on the mission. Many of them had tried to flee on a number of occasions, but they were essentially treated as slaves. While some enjoyed the lifestyle on the mission, many did not and fought hard for their independence. They were overjoyed when they were freed and happy to be free to worship as they pleased and live as they wanted.

A Secular Town

On July 29, 1841, San Juan Capistrano was officially assigned as a secular Mexican town by Governor Juan Alvarado. Anyone who still lived on the mission (and they were very few people at this time) was granted land to use as their own. At this point, the land and the town now looked completely different than they had when San Juan Capistrano was a mission in full swing. It was now a town that was barely hanging on for survival, and many complained that it had turned into an area where unsavory characters resided.

A mere four years later, in 1846, the property of the mission was auctioned off for just $710 worth of hides and tallow (this would be similar to about $15,000 today) to an Englishman named John Forster and his partner James McKinley. This was a very small amount of money for such an historic piece of land. Many people believe that this deal was not very fair. The governor of Mexico that sold the land, Governor Pio Pico, sold it to his brother-in-law John Forster. People believed that had Pico sold the land to someone else, it might have been preserved better and he would have sold it for more money. As it was, the families of Forster and McKinley took up residence at San Juan Capistrano, as did others, in the mission buildings. Until this time, there was still a priest living on the mission, but he left in late 1842, leaving the mission without a priest for the first time ever since it had been settled.

With no priest living on the mission, the very first secular priest took charge. His name was reverend José Maria Rosáles, and he took over in 1843. At this point, it was safe to say that the mission was a completely different place than what it had been a mere 40 years before. The Fathers had all left and the land and the society of San Juan Capistrano was a completely different place than it had ever been before.

Chapter 4: History of the California Statehood

For the next five years, there was a lot of fighting between the Mexicans in California and the United States settlers that wanted to take over the land and make it a United States territory. The Mexican American War was fought, and the end result saw a new government take over for California. In 1848, the Unites States won the Mexican American War and signed the Treaty of Guadalupe Hidalgo. This treaty granted California and the other western territories to the United States. The great gold rush was just beginning, which brought millions of American settlers out west to California and the other territories. Due to this great migration and the new government, the Mission San Juan Capistrano was set to see another large set of changes.

In 1850, the United States declared the territory of California a state. A large number of parishioners and diocese that settled the area or had remained there during the political strife of the last few years were now petitioning the government to return the mission buildings and lands in California to the church. It made many of these people very sad to see the state of these missions and they wanted to restore them to what they once were. A large number of the missions were falling apart and were virtually unusable, while others had been turned into stores, inns, horse stables and bars.

The missions were given back to the Catholic Church by President Abraham Lincoln in response to the outcries by the many parishioners and Catholics that lived in the area. Many of these people began to work hard to rebuild the missions, including Mission San Juan Capistrano, to what they once were in their heyday. They began to rebuild the buildings and restore many of the areas that had once been places of worship for their ancestors.

During the time between the late 1870s and the early 1900s, a large movement of artistic people began to take an interest in the abandoned missions. Artists, photographers and others visionaries came to the missions to take photographs and to paint the land as they saw it. This helped to spread the word of the mission across the country and to tell others about the plight of the abandoned missions. Massive restoration campaigns were waged, with many wealthy people donating large sums of money to help to rebuild the many neglected missions.

In 1910, Father O'Sullivan began restoring the Mission San Juan Capistrano. He worked with his own bare hands to bring the nearly unrecognizable mission back to what it once was. He carved the windows, made the beams and started the important restoration of the historical site of Mission San Juan Capistrano. He also worked with the Landmarks Club of California to raise money to help with his restoration of the mission. As he worked, others came to join his as well and by the time he died in 1933, the mission was looking more like it had in the years when it was thriving. Restoration of San Juan Capistrano continued on for many years and helped to spark more interest in the Mission among the people in town.

Chapter 5: What Was Life on the Mission Like During the Mission Period?

Restoration
San Juan Capistrano
Kincade

Life on Mission San Juan Capistrano was blessed because everyone was working together and fostering a sense of family, but it certainly was not easy! If you did not have all of the things that you can simply go to a store and buy today, how would you get your food and the things that you needed to live? As you can guess, the Fathers and the Native American converts (called neophytes) at the mission had to fend for themselves when it came to food, water, clothing, transportation and everything else that is required of everyday life. They could not head to the nearest Target or Wal-Mart to stock up on what they needed, so they did what they could with the natural resources that they had.

Imports

One of the most important things to the success of the mission, especially in the early years, was the generous donations and other imported goods that came from New Spain and other missions. Farming successfully and raising animals is not an overnight process. You cannot expect to plant some crops and have them ready to eat in a matter of days! This means that the people on the mission struggled very much in the first few years because they had to wait for their crops to take off and their animals to grow as well. During this growing and learning phase, other missions and the ships from Spain would bring items such as food and clothing to those who were living on the Mission San Juan Capistrano. This helped to get them through until the mission was fully self-sufficient.

Daily Work

For the most part, life on the mission was filled with hard work, religion, and spending time with family and community members. Young boys and adult males who were Native American converts or immigrant Europeans living on the mission would spend a lot of time every single day tending to the farm and the animals. The main crops to be farmed were barley, maize and wheat. Cattle, sheep, goats, and horses were among the large amount of livestock that lived on the mission. The sustaining force on the mission was the farmland and so it was very important that they keep the farm running at all times. The neophyte workers were the main workers on the farm and did the brunt of the work. They had to be up at dawn to begin tending to the fields and feeding the livestock. Their jobs were very hard and filled with physical labor.

The amount of work on the farm that the natives had to do was far different than what they were used to. They were used to working as much as they could for the day until they were tired and then resting when they needed to. The pace at the mission was strenuous, however, and the workers were not given the rest that they so desperately wanted and needed. They were forced to work all day long, with the exception of the times when they would pray or take their meal breaks. Because many of the neophyte workers were unhappy with how much work they had to do and the fact that their schedule was made by someone else, they often became restless and attempted to run away.

The young boys would follow in the footsteps of their fathers and work hard on the farms as well. They were an integral part of getting all of the crops planted, watered and then pulled. Their only education was what they got on the job and during church, so they did not attend a traditional school.

The men and boys that did not work on the farms were often put to work on building structures and adding on to adobes and buildings that were already in existence. For nearly 10 years, there was an abundance of work to be done on the construction of the Great Stone Church. This church took a large amount of time and massive amounts of work to construct, so it kept the men very, very busy.

In order to complete the construction on the many buildings found on the mission, the workers had to first fabricate their own construction materials. There were carpentry workers that used various methods to create beams, lintels and a number of other structural elements that were important to daily life. Artisanal workers carved furniture and doors out of wood to be used in the construction of living structures and other buildings as well. Bricks were also used and were fired in large ovens in order to make them strong and last longer. Those workers who spent time firing bricks also used the ovens to make dishes and glazed ceramic pots for eating and drinking.

The Fathers spent all of their time instructing on the Catholic faith. Their job was to teach all of the young children their daily lessons and to also mentor the new converts. All of the new converts were to learn about the faith and to spend a large amount of time everyday learning about the Bible. The Fathers also spent much of their daily life performing baptisms and weddings.

The women on the mission spent their time helping in the fields as well as cooking, cleaning, and making clothing. They were also expected to raise the children, so they had a large amount of daily duties! The women did not do any of the physical labor on the mission, as it was their job to see to it that everyone was clothed and fed. They also made candles, soap and special ointments out of animal fat. This was very important to the everyday life of the mission, as they needed soap to keep clean and candles to see with. They also could trade these items in order to obtain things that they might not have on the mission.

Each day, young girls would attend lessons at the church on the Bible and their religion. After completion of their lessons they would do their chores. Usually, they would work side-by-side with their mothers and the other women on the mission. They would learn to cook and clean, as well as make clothing and knit.

Whether you were male or female, young or old, your life on the mission was filled with strenuous work. Can you imagine how tired they must have been at the end of the night?

Important Industries for Trade

In addition to farming, which was vital for the people of the mission to do in order to eat and live, there were other industries that helped the mission to make enough money to sustain the society. Olives were grown prevalently on the land, and thus making olive oil was very important to make money for the mission. Someone had to grow the olives, cure them and then press them under massive stone wheels in order to make olive oil. Once made, the oil could be traded to other missions and to people in surrounding areas in order to access items that were not available on the mission land.

Grapes were also grown prevalently and were used to make wine. The grapes had to be grown and then fermented. Once they were made into wine, the wine could be used in religious ceremonies and it could also be used in trade to other areas. The grapes were actually called "Mission" grapes and the wine that was produced was highly sought after by neighboring areas.

How Did they Get Water?

You know that they moved the settlement to be closer to water, but do you know how they made that water purified for drinking and cleaning? Water is obviously a very important element to all life and the people on the mission needed it for cooking, cleaning, bathing and drinking. They had to take the water from the two nearby rivers and make it useful to their needs. They did this by building three very long aqueducts through the very central courtyard of the mission. This directed the water right into the community, where it was collected into large cisterns. There, the water was filtered so that it could be used for the everyday needs of the people on the mission. It was quite a process to get fresh water back then; a lot different than just turning on the tap!

Living Arrangements

Those who lived on San Juan Capistrano stayed in various quarters depending upon their marital status and their age. The Fathers slept in the main living quarters in the main quadrant, along with the European immigrants that they travelled with. The Native American converts were divided into various groups for living and sleeping.

Couples that were married and their small children lived in their own smaller "village," which was very close to the central portion of the mission's quadrant. When the mission was first established these village homes were usually Native American domed huts, but as the mission grew, the residences were made from adobe.

There was a women's living quarters for those women who were eight years old or older and were not married, or women who were widowed. This was a dormitory style room. The door was locked in order to keep these women protected while they were sleeping.

Young men and boys also had their own men's quarters where they all slept, only their door was not locked, as it was not believed that they needed protection.

Religion and Learning

You can imagine that religion was a very large part of the everyday life of the people on the mission. The entire point of the Mission San Juan Capistrano was to spread the Catholic faith to the natives of the area and to establish a thriving religious center. Because of this, religious learning was the cornerstone of every single day. Everyone spent a large amount of time in church services, where they would pray and listen to the sermons of the Fathers.

They would also sing songs and perform religious ceremonies in order to celebrate various saints or to commemorate important dates in history. The Fathers ran all of the church ceremonies and were instrumental in encouraging all of the people to read the Bible more and study Catholicism.

Mass was held twice a day at the Serra Chapel, however from 1806 to 1812 this was held in the Great Stone Church. The services are probably not what you would imagine if you are comparing them to the services that you attend at your place of worship today. The Native American converts did not have the comfort of pews like we do today. Instead, they would stand during the service or they would kneel on the ground. The Europeans who were uneducated and the Native American converts did not always understand the services, because they were held completely in Latin.

Music was a large part of Mass because of the many musical talents that the Native Americans possessed. They used various musical instruments to play hymns and to create new spiritual songs that added immensely to the beauty and celebration of Mass.

When the Great Stone Church was completed, there was a huge sense of pride among the converted Natives and the European immigrants. They had all contributed to the construction of this massive church, and they all lent their talents in painting and decorating the interior of the church as well.

Marriages and Other Ceremonies

If you wanted to get married, get baptized, or you needed someone in your family buried, you were definitely in the right place at Mission San Juan Capistrano! With multiple Fathers in residence, there was always someone there to perform these very important rites of passage and to bless them. Father Mugártegui blessed the very first Native American marriage on January 23, 1777. The day was deemed the feast of the "Espousals of the Blessed Virgin Mary." Father Mugártegui was also the same priest that presided over the first burial ceremony on the Mission in 1781.

In order for any couple to be married, they must have been baptized. Only those Native American converts that were baptized were able to participate in a marriage ceremony.

Marriages were a large religious celebration at Mission San Juan Capistrano. First the couple was officially married and blessed, and a full High Mass ceremony was held. The bells were rung and then everyone would feast as a toast to the married couple. While there was not as much of a party atmosphere as marriages today, there was music and some dancing. The most important aspect of the marriage was the blessing and the prayers, and these were done by everyone at the mission.

The baptisms that were held at San Juan Capistrano were extremely important. If a Native American wanted to live on the mission, he had to become baptized. Once baptized, he had committed himself to the mission and was an integral part of the society. Even if he decided he wanted to leave, after baptism he had made a strong commitment to the mission and was therefore not able to leave.

Every single marriage, baptism, and burial was recorded and all of these have been preserved on the grounds of the mission today.

What Kinds of Food Did they Eat?

They definitely did not have McDonald's on the mission, or any of the other popular restaurants and supermarkets that we have today. Other than food that was imported from other missions or from Spain, the Mission San Juan Capistrano farmed and raised all of their own food. They were fortunate to have started their mission in the sunshine and fertile soil of California, and this made it possible for them to have success with a large amount of different crops. Grains, wheat, beans, peaches, figs, walnuts, grapes, pears, oranges, olives, dates palms, corn and many other vegetables all grew plentiful in the area, and this provided the people on the mission with the many foods that they needed to survive.

Animals, such as cattle and chicken, were raised and thus the mission was provided with milk and meat. They were able to enjoy chicken or beef on rare occasions, yet they mainly lived on vegetables and grains.

For breakfast, the most commonly served meal was called Atole. This was a special type of soup made from barley and a number of other healthful grains. It was said to give the mission residents plenty of strength to get through the hard work that the day was sure to bring. You might be thinking soup for breakfast sounds odd, but they did not have cereal or waffles back then! They also needed a meal that was hearty enough to last them all the way through the morning, as they had no snack break during the daytime hours.

Dinner (or lunch as we call it) usually consisted of another healthful soup called Pozole. This was a thicker, pastier soup that was filled with beans and peas. It was said to give the many people on the mission the strength that they needed to get through the second half of their long day.

Supper was usually Atole once again, as it was prevalent and easy to make. While the residents of the mission most often ate Atole and Pozole, for special events and religious ceremonies they were able to have more fanciful food items. While they certainly did not have candy or chocolate cake, they did have sweets made from the fruits that grew in the area. They also made wine, which was drunk at only the most special of occasions.

Games and Fun

It's safe to say that games and fun were a very small part of the everyday life on the mission. Establishing the land and getting everything up and running was the most important task at hand, and even the children were expected to participate in activities that helped to grow the society and spread the word of Christianity. Can you imagine a life without very much fun or play?

The children did find some ways to enjoy themselves while on the mission. They had many handmade toys that they played with, such as dolls made of fabric and yarn, and toys that were fashioned from clay. They did not have a large amount of free time to play, but when they did have some time they spent it using these toys.

The native children and the European immigrants on the mission also enjoyed singing songs together and playing with crude instruments that they had. This was probably one of the most popular pastimes among the children at San Juan Capistrano, and it helped them to advance their musical skills and to become closer to their newfound friends. Dancing was also a fun way for the children to let loose and be free after a full day of work and religious lessons.

Medicine and Healing

During the late 1700s and early 1800s, very little was known about the spread of disease, and the birth of modern medicine would not come for many years. Because of this, disease wiped out hundreds and thousands of people at the mission and in the surrounding San Francisco Bay area. The Europeans brought over many diseases that the Native Americans had never been exposed to before, and because their bodies had not built up the necessary immunity, many Native Americans died.

Disease also reached epidemic status on the mission grounds because of the close quarters that everyone lived in. If one person got sick in the small room where many people lived, they could all be sick within a matter of days. There was an especially dangerous epidemic from 1806-1810, when one out of every four Native Americans died in the San Francisco Bay area.

Because little was known about medicine, a lot of the healing tactics that were used involved prayer and blessings. The Fathers would stand over the ailing and the sick members of the mission and say prayers for them, asking for them to become better. This was really the best that they could do at this time, because they did not have the many different medicines and treatments that we have today.

They also used natural remedies such as herbs and plants to help to heal the sick during this time. Some were more useful than others. When someone got a very dangerous disease such as measles or smallpox, the chances of survival were very slim.

The Mission Bells

You probably have a bell at your school, or some other sound that goes off when it is time for you to switch to another class or to go home at the end of the day. The people on the Mission San Juan Capistrano used a similar system. Because they used every minute of every day and lived a regimented life, they needed to stay on schedule. They used the large Mission bells that had been on the mission since its founding to signal events. Every single morning, the bells would ring at sunrise to awaken everyone for the day. There was no sleeping in on the mission! This bell told them to get out of bed and head to Mass for their morning prayers. Afterwards, they would go to breakfast for 45 minutes and then off to work.

After their morning of work, the bells would ring to signal that everyone was to gather for dinner (which is what we call lunch). After lunch and a quick break the bell would ring again so that everyone would know to get back to work! They certainly did not spend any of their days being lazy, and the bells kept everyone on their toes and alert. The bell would be rung again at the end of the work day, letting them all know that it was time for supper and then bed.

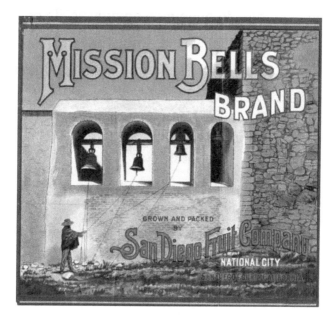

The bells were also a very important part of the many religious ceremonies on the mission. As you know, the mission was founded in order to spread the word of Christianity in general and Catholicism in particular, and so there were many different ceremonies held on a regular basis. When the bells were sounded, this often meant that a special event was occurring, like a marriage or baptism, or that High Mass was being held. During births and funerals the bells were also rung to announce an arriving life or to announce one that was leaving. They also rang the bells when a ship was arriving with goods or people, or when a missionary was coming or going.

The original bells hung on a tree on the mission property for more than 15 years, until the very large and impressive bell tower was constructed in 1791. Four more bells were dedicated over the years and inscribed with Latin phrases, blessing them as the San Juan Capistrano bells. After the 1812 earthquake, the two largest bells were cracked and their sound was forever altered, but they were still kept in memory of what they once were.

When the New Mission Church was elevated to Basilica status in 2000, exact replicas of the cracked bells were created and they replaced the old ones on display at the rebuilt Mission San Juan Capistrano.

Chapter 6: Modern Day

Throughout the 1950s and beyond, huge fundraising drives were held to help raise even more money for the restoration of the Mission San Juan Capistrano. Nearly everything was rebuilt and given a beautiful facelift. A school was opened on the grounds of the mission in the 1950s, and sidewalks were also built all through the mission land. Beams and arches were renovated to replicate what they had once looked like, and the Serra Chapel was also restored to its original splendor. The altar was redone in shining gold leaf and people began to visit more regularly.

The Great Stone Church has also been updated, and a stabilization program was started in 1987 so that they can continue to preserve this historic church. Can you believe that a church that was once built in the early 1800s has survived the many earthquakes that have ravaged Southern California? The Great Stone Church is a reminder to everyone in the area of the lasting legacy of the Mission San Juan Capistrano.

These days, the many buildings of the mission are used for different things. There is a very cool museum area that shows off some of the tools that were used by the people that settled the mission hundreds of years ago, as well as displays about the agricultural and industrial influence of the mission people. Visitors are always welcome to the museum and the other areas of the mission, so if you ever get a chance to go there, you should! You will get to see firsthand the many interesting artifacts from the working mission more than 200 years ago.

The Serra Chapel is still in full swing on the mission property. In many ways, the chapel and the rest of the mission are still a very big part of the community. Things are of course very different than they were 200 years ago, but San Juan Capistrano is still a center for the town and a lot still goes on there. It is an active parish that serves the larger city of San Juan Capistrano and is a beautiful place to spend time.

One very large event is held every year on the grounds of the Mission San Juan Capistrano. This event is called the Return of the Swallows and it begins each year on March 19th. The swallows, which are a type of bird, fly south every single winter, but they always return on March 19th to San Juan Capistrano. They never come a day late or a day early and so their arrival draws huge crowds. People come to greet them each year on the grounds of the mission. This event has become one that thousands look forward to each year as the flocks of swallows descend on the town. People bring their picnics and blankets and sit on the grounds to watch for the swallows in eager anticipation.

San Juan Capistrano has been restored beautifully and is now well taken care of. In fact, the historic mission is now known as "Jewel of the Missions," for its stunning architecture and many pieces of American history.

Conclusion

The Mission San Juan Capistrano is filled with a great amount of history. We can learn a lot from the people that settled the mission, as they worked hard for something that they truly believed in. The Mission San Juan Capistrano is now a place that is filled with culture and rich history. What have you learned from the history and the trials and tribulations of the Mission San Juan Capistrano? If anything, you know how hard it was for anyone to set up a new community in the Wild West in the early 1800s, and you have a great appreciation for the hearty settlers of that time.

Additional Resources

- California Missions On-Line Project

  http://www.cuca.k12.ca.us/lessons/missions/Capistrano/SanJuanCapistrano.html#use

  This is a student project posted online that offers interesting and factual information about various California missions, including San Juan Capistrano.

- Mission San Juan Capistrano Home Page

  http://missionsjc.com/

  The historic landmark and museum home page offers visitor information, events information and a large amount of factual information on the mission.

- The San Juan Capistrano Historical Society

  http://www.sjchistoricalsociety.com/missionsjc.html

  The goal of the San Juan Capistrano Historical Society website is to spread the word about the town of San Juan Capistrano and its history.

- The Spanish Missions of California, Mission San Juan Capistrano Page

  http://www.californias-missions.org/individual/mission_sjc.htm

  This site offers detailed information about the many California missions. The site's goal is to give teachers and students resources for learning more about the history of the missions.

- Wikipedia: Mission San Juan Capistrano Page

http://en.wikipedia.org/wiki/Mission_San_J
uan_Capistrano#Mission_Period_.281769
.E2.80.931833.29

This independently written article on Mission San Juan Capistrano offers a wealth of information on the founding and history of the mission.

CPSIA information can be obtained at www.ICGtesting.com
Printed in the USA
LVOW01s0305230315

431606LV00029B/606/P